Investigations

Pushing

Patricia Whitehouse

Heinemann Library
Chicago, Illinois

Customer Service 888-454-2279
Visit our website at www.heinemannlibrary.com

Designed by Sue Emerson, Heinemann Library; Page layout by Que-Net Media
Printed and bound in the United States by Lake Book Manufacturing, Inc.
Photo research by Beth Chisholm

07 06 05 04 03
10 9 8 7 6 5 4 3 2 1

Library of Congress Cataloging-in-Publication Data
Whitehouse, Patricia, 1958-
  Pushing / Patricia Whitehouse.
       p. cm. – (Investigations)
Includes index.
Summary: Presents simple hands-on experiments that demonstrate what can make pushing easier or more difficult.
  ISBN: 1-4034-0908-0 (HC), 1-4034-3469-7 (Pbk.)
 1. Force and energy–Juvenile literature. 2. Power (Mechanics)–Juvenile literature. 3. Force and energy–Experiments–Juvenile literature. 4. Power (Mechanics)–Experiments–Juvenile literature. [1. Force and energy–Experiments. 2. Power (Mechanics)–Experiments. 3. Experiments.] I. Title.
  QC73.4 .W475 2003
  531'.6–dc21

                                2002014424

Acknowledgments
The author and publishers are grateful to the following for permission to reproduce copyright material:
pp. 4, 5, 6, 7, 8, 9, 10, 11, 12, 13, 14, 15, 16, 17, 22, 23, 24 Que-Net/Heinemann Library; pp. 18, 19, 20, 21 Robert Lifson/Heinemann Library; back cover (L-R) Robert Lifson/Heinemann Library, Que-Net/Heinemann Library

Cover photograph by Que-Net/Heinemann Library

Special thanks to our advisory panel for their help in the preparation of this book:

Alice Bethke,
Library Consultant
Palo Alto, CA

Eileen Day,
Preschool Teacher
Chicago, IL

Kathleen Gilbert,
Second Grade Teacher
Round Rock, TX

Sandra Gilbert,
Library Media Specialist
Fiest Elementary School
Houston, TX

Jan Gobeille, Kindergarten Teacher
Garfield Elementary
Oakland, CA

Angela Leeper,
Educational Consultant
North Carolina Department
of Public Instruction
Wake Forest, NC

Some words are shown in bold, **like this.**
You can find them in the picture glossary on page 23.

Contents

What Is Pushing? 4

How Hard Do You Have to Push? . . . 6

Can You Push Something
  Heavier Than You?. 10

Which Handle Can Push?. 14

Can You Push Down to
  Push Something Up?. 18

Quiz 22

Picture Glossary. 23

Note to Parents and Teachers 24

Answer to Quiz. 24

Index. 24

What Is Pushing?

Pushing is one way to move something away from you.

You can push a stroller to move it.

Some things are easy to push.

Other things are hard to push.

How Hard Do You Have to Push?

The **climber** is heavy.

You need to push it into the corner.

Push the climber.

You have to push hard to move it over the **rough** carpet.

Now the **climber** is on the
smooth floor.

Will you have to push hard now?

You only have to push a little.

The climber is easier to push on a smooth floor.

Can You Push Something Heavier Than You?

You dropped your crayons under the chair.

Can you move the chair to get them?

Try to push the chair.

It is too heavy for you.

Ask a friend to help you.

Together you can push the chair.

More people means more
push power.

Now you can color with all
the crayons!

Which Handle Can Push?

Pieces of paper are on the floor.

You need to clean up.

You can push the paper with
a broom.

Will a **handle** help?

A rope **handle** will not work.

The rope will not stay straight.

A wooden handle will stay straight.

You need a straight handle
for pushing.

Can You Push Down to Push Something Up?

This is a **pogo stick**.

You can balance on it.

Jump down on the pogo stick.

What happens?

When you push down, the
pogo stick goes up.

The harder you push down on the pogo stick, the higher you bounce up.

Quiz

Will it be harder to push the toy through the **rough** sand or on the **smooth** floor?

Look for the answer on page 24.

Picture Glossary

climber
pages 6, 7, 8, 9

handle
pages 15, 16, 17

pogo stick
pages 18, 19, 20, 21

rough
pages 7, 22

smooth
pages 8, 9, 22

Note to Parents and Teachers

In physics, force is defined as a push or a pull. This book offers children an opportunity to explore the physical laws of pushing in terms they can understand. Simple experiments demonstrate that the amount of force needed to push an object depends on the size of the object and the type of surface it moves along. Children will also find out that pushes can change direction—pushing down can push something up.

Read the first two pages of each chapter, and help children think of a solution to the chapter's question. For example, after reading pages 10 and 11, have the children try to move a chair that is heavier than they are. Then read pages 12 and 13 and discuss whether your solution matched the one in the book or how it was different.

 CAUTION: Children should not attempt any experiment without an adult's permission and help.

Index

chair 10, 11, 12
climber 6, 7, 8, 9
crayons 10, 13
handle 15, 16, 17
paper 14, 15
pogo stick . . 18, 19, 20, 21
rope 16

Answer to quiz on page 22

The toy is harder to push in the **rough** sand.